The Little Book of Big Emojis 2024

Second Edition

Published by Beyond Pages
Loveld 48, Pellenberg, Belgium

Second edition

For inquiries, please contact:

Beyond Pages
Loveld 48
Pellenberg, Belgium
Email: beyondpages9@gmail.com

ISBN: 9798873780921

Emoji Index

4

DESCRIPTION:
REPRESENTS A BIG SMILE,
INDICATING HAPPINESS OR AMUSEMENT.

EXAMPLE:
"I'M LOOKING FORWARD TO THE WEEKEND! "

DESCRIPTION:
FEATURES A BIG SMILE AND CLOSED,
JOYFUL EYES. SUGGESTS GENUINE HAPPINESS OR
THAT SOMETHING IS FUNNY.

EXAMPLE:
"THAT'S HILARIOUS! "

DESCRIPTION:
DISPLAYS A WIDE, TOOTHY SMILE.
OFTEN CONVEYS ENTHUSIASTIC
HAPPINESS OR EXCITEMENT.

EXAMPLE:
"THIS IS FANTASTIC NEWS! "

DESCRIPTION:
SHOWS A BROAD, TOOTHY SMILE WITH CLOSED EYE
SUGGESTING SOMETHING IS
VERY FUNNY OR AMUSING.

EXAMPLE:
"I CAN'T STOP LAUGHING! "

DESCRIPTION:
REPRESENTS A EMOTIONAL SMILE,
CAN ALSO INDICATE FINDING
SOMETHING OR SOMEONE CUTE.

EXAMPLE:
"THANK YOU FOR THE GIFT "

DESCRIPTION:
SHOWS A SMILE WITH A DROP OF SWEAT,
TYPICALLY USED TO CONVEY A SENSE OF RELIEF,
NERVOUSNESS, OR BEING IN A SWEATY OR
HOT SITUATION. IT CAN ALSO SUGGEST THAT SOMEO
IS FEELING AWKWARD OR EMBARRASSED.

EXAMPLE:
"WHEW, I BARELY MADE IT ON TIME! "

DESCRIPTION:

REPRESENTS LAUGHTER THAT IS SO HEARTY THAT TEARS ARE STREAMING FROM THE EYES. IT'S ONE OF THE MOST WIDELY USED EMOJIS AND TYPICALLY INDICATES THAT SOMETHING IS EXTREMELY FUNNY..

EXAMPLE:

"I LAUGHED SO HARD I CRIED! 😂"

DESCRIPTION:

DEPICTS A FACE LAUGHING SO HARD THAT IT'S ROLLING ON THE FLOOR. IT'S AN EXAGGERATED VERSION OF "FACE WITH TEARS OF JOY" AND CONVEYS INTENSE HUMOR OR AMUSEMENT.

EXAMPLE:

"THAT JOKE WAS TOO MUCH; I'M ROLLING! "

DESCRIPTION:

REPRESENTS MIXED FEELINGS OF HAPPINESS AND SADNESS. THE TEAR CAN INDICATE THAT THERE'S AN EMOTIONAL LAYER TO THE JOY, POSSIBLY NOSTALGIA OR RELIEF.

EXAMPLE:

"THINKING OF OLD MEMORIES MAKES ME SMILE AND TEAR UP. "

DESCRIPTION:

A CLASSIC SMILEY FACE. REPRESENTS A CONTENT, PLEASED, OR RELAXED EXPRESSION. LESS INTENSE THAN OTHER SMILEY EMOJIS, BUT STILL WARM AND POSITIVE.

EXAMPLE:

"I HAD A PEACEFUL DAY. 🙂"

DESCRIPTION:

INDICATES HAPPINESS, WARMTH, OR CONTENTMENT. THE CLOSED EYES GIVE IT A MORE INTIMATE, BLUSHING FEELING, OFTEN SUGGESTING GENUINE PLEASURE OR GRATITUDE.

EXAMPLE:

"THANK YOU FOR THE GIFT; I LOVE IT! "

DESCRIPTION:

REPRESENTS INNOCENCE OR ANGELIC BEHAVIOR OFTEN USED WHEN SOMEONE IS FEELING SAINTLY OR JUST DID A GOOD DEED.

EXAMPLE:

"I HELPED MY NEIGHBOR WITH THEIR GROCERIES TODAY.

DESCRIPTION:

REPRESENTS SILLINESS, SARCASM, OR A PLAYFUL SENSE OF IRONY. IT CAN INDICATE THAT SOMETHING IS NOT MEANT TO BE TAKEN TOO SERIOUSLY OR MIGHT BE THE OPPOSITE OF WHAT'S EXPECTED.

EXAMPLE:

"WELL, THAT WENT AS PLANNED... NOT. 🙃"

DESCRIPTION:

CONVEYS A PLAYFUL OR TEASING TONE, OFTEN USED TO ADD A JOKING OR FLIRTATIOUS NUANCE TO A MESSAGE.

EXAMPLE:

"MAYBE I HAVE A SURPRISE FOR YOU. "

DESCRIPTION:

INDICATES FEELINGS OF RELIEF, PEACE, OR RELAXATION. IT CAN BE USED WHEN SOMEONE FEELS AT EASE AFTER A STRESSFUL SITUATION OR IS CONTENT WITH HOW THINGS ARE GOING.

EXAMPLE:

"FINALLY DONE WITH MY EXAMS! 😌"

DESCRIPTION:

REPRESENTS STRONG AFFECTION OR ADMIRATION, OFTEN USED WHEN SOMEONE FINDS SOMETHING OR SOMEONE VERY ATTRACTIVE OR APPEALING.

EXAMPLE:

"LOOK AT THAT ADORABLE PUPPY! "

DESCRIPTION:

CONVEYS A WARM, FUZZY FEELING, OFTEN ASSOCIATED WITH LOVE, AFFECTION, OR BEING TOUCHED BY A GESTURE.

EXAMPLE:

"I'M SO GRATEFUL FOR MY FRIENDS. "

DESCRIPTION:

REPRESENTS SENDING LOVE OR AFFECTION, OFTEN USED AS A GESTURE OF FONDNESS WHEN SAYING GOODBYE OR SHOWING APPRECIATION.

EXAMPLE:

"MISS YOU ALREADY! "

DESCRIPTION:
INDICATES A KISS OR AFFECTION, BUT IT'S MORE NEUTRAL AND LESS INTENSE THAN THE "FACE BLOWING A KISS" EMOJI.

EXAMPLE:
"THANKS FOR THE HELP. "

DESCRIPTION:
CONVEYS WARMTH, AFFECTION, OR FONDNESS, SIMILAR TO THE KISSING FACE BUT WITH A MORE INTIMATE OR GENUINE FEELING DUE TO THE CLOSED EYES.

EXAMPLE:
"YOU'RE SUCH A DEAR FRIEND. "

DESCRIPTION:
REPRESENTS HUNGER, A TASTE FOR SOMETHING, OR ENJOYING WHAT ONE IS EATING. THE TONGUE STICKING OUT CAN ALSO INDICATE PLAYFUL CHEEKINESS.

EXAMPLE:
"THIS ICE CREAM IS DELICIOUS! "

DESCRIPTION:
DEPICTS A PLAYFUL OR TEASING TONE DUE TO THE TONGUE STICKING OUT. CAN INDICATE SILLINESS OR BE USED TO LIGHTEN THE MOOD.

EXAMPLE:
"GUESS WHO ATE THE LAST COOKIE? "

DESCRIPTION:
REPRESENTS PLAYFUL HUMOR OR LIGHT-HEARTEDNESS. THE SQUINTING EYES COMBINED WITH THE TONGUE CAN ALSO INDICATE SOMEONE IS BEING CHEEKY OR PLAYFUL.

EXAMPLE:
"YOU CAN'T CATCH ME! "

DESCRIPTION:
CONVEYS A PLAYFUL, WINKING GESTURE COMBINED WITH A STICKING-OUT TONGUE, OFTEN USED TO TEASE OR JOKE.

EXAMPLE:
"GOTCHA! JUST KIDDING. "

DESCRIPTION:

SHOWS A CRAZY, SILLY EXPRESSION. ONE EYE IS LARGER THAN THE OTHER, GIVING IT A ZANY, WILD FEELING. REPRESENTS GOOFINESS OR WACKINESS.

EXAMPLE:

"IT'S BEEN A WILD DAY! "

DESCRIPTION:

EXPRESSES SKEPTICISM, DISBELIEF, OR MILD DISAPPROVAL. THE RAISED EYEBROW GIVES IT AN INQUISITIVE OR DOUBTFUL APPEARANCE.

EXAMPLE:

"REALLY? ARE YOU SURE ABOUT THAT? "

DESCRIPTION:

REPRESENTS DEEP THOUGHT OR ANALYZING SOMETHING CRITICALLY. THE MONOCLE IS A CLASSIC SYMBOL OF SCRUTINY OR BEING DISCERNING.

EXAMPLE:

"LET ME TAKE A CLOSER LOOK AT THIS. "

DESCRIPTION:
CELEBRATES GEEK CULTURE, SHOWING THICK BLACK
GLASSES AND BUCK TEETH. OFTEN USED IN THE
CONTEXT OF READING, STUDYING, OR ANYTHING
RELATED TO ACADEMICS AND KNOWLEDGE.

EXAMPLE:
"TIME TO DIVE INTO THIS NEW BOOK! "

DESCRIPTION:
EXPRESSES A COOL, RELAXED VIBE. OFTEN USED
TO CONVEY CONFIDENCE OR TO INDICATE THAT
SOMEONE IS FEELING "COOL" ABOUT SOMETHING.

EXAMPLE:
"BEACH DAY! TIME TO RELAX AND CHILL. "

DESCRIPTION:
REPRESENTS BEING UNDERCOVER,
SNEAKY, OR IN DISGUISE.

EXAMPLE:
"GOING UNDERCOVER FOR THE SURPRISE PARTY.
THEY WON'T RECOGNIZE ME!"

DESCRIPTION:
EYES ARE DEPICTED AS STARS, EXPRESSING EXCITEMENT, ADMIRATION, OR BEING "WOWED" BY SOMETHING AMAZING.

EXAMPLE:
"THAT CONCERT WAS PHENOMENAL! "

DESCRIPTION:
FESTIVE AND CELEBRATORY, COMPLETE WITH A PARTY HORN AND CONFETTI. OFTEN USED FOR BIRTHDAYS, NEW YEAR'S, OR ANY CELEBRATORY EVENT.

EXAMPLE:
"HAPPY BIRTHDAY TO ME! "

DESCRIPTION:
SUGGESTS A SLY, SMUG, MISCHIEVOUS, OR SUGGESTIVE SENTIMENT. MAY ALSO IMPLY CONFIDENCE OR SATISFACTION.

EXAMPLE:
"I KNEW YOU'D COME AROUND. "

DESCRIPTION:
SHOWS DISSATISFACTION OR DISINTEREST. OFTEN USED TO EXPRESS SKEPTICISM, MILD ANNOYANCE OR BEING UNDERWHELMED.

EXAMPLE:
"NOT THIS AGAIN... 😒"

DESCRIPTION:
EXPRESSES SADNESS, REGRET, OR DISAPPOINTMENT THE DOWNTURNED EYEBROWS AND MOUTH CONVEY A SENSE OF MILD UNHAPPINESS.

EXAMPLE:
"I WAS REALLY HOPING FOR BETTER NEWS. 😞"

DESCRIPTION:
CONVEYS A SENSE OF DEEP THOUGHT OR REFLECTION, OFTEN USED TO SIGNIFY FEELING SAD OR REGRETFUL ABOUT SOMETHING.

EXAMPLE:
"THINKING ABOUT OLD TIMES... 😔"

DESCRIPTION:
REPRESENTS A HIGH DEGREE OF CONCERN OR WORRY.

EXAMPLE:
"I HOPE EVERYONE IS OKAY AFTER THAT STORM. "

DESCRIPTION:
SHOWS UNCERTAINTY OR CONFUSION, OFTEN USED WHEN SOMEONE DOESN'T UNDERSTAND OR ISN'T SURE ABOUT SOMETHING.

EXAMPLE:
"I'M NOT SURE WHAT YOU MEAN. "

DESCRIPTION:
A MILDER VERSION OF SADNESS OR DISPLEASURE, LESS INTENSE THAN THE FULL FROWN.

EXAMPLE:
"IT'S A BIT CLOUDY TODAY. "

DESCRIPTION:
REPRESENTS MORE PRONOUNCED FEELINGS OF UNHAPPINESS OR DISSATISFACTION.

EXAMPLE:
"I WISH THINGS WERE DIFFERENT. 🙁"

DESCRIPTION:
CONVEYS MODERATE PAIN, STRUGGLE, OR FRUSTRATION.

EXAMPLE:
"TRYING SO HARD BUT IT'S JUST NOT WORKING OUT. 😣"

DESCRIPTION:
REPRESENTS FRUSTRATION OR CONFUSION, OFTEN DUE TO A CHALLENGING OR OVERWHELMING SITUATION.

EXAMPLE:
"I CAN'T BELIEVE THIS HAPPENED AGAIN. "

DESCRIPTION:
REPRESENTS FEELINGS OF EXHAUSTION OR EXASPERATION.

EXAMPLE:
"IT'S BEEN SUCH A LONG DAY, I'M BEAT. "

DESCRIPTION:
A MORE EXAGGERATED DISPLAY OF FATIGUE OR DESPAIR. IT CAN SIGNIFY BEING WORN OUT OR DEEPLY FRUSTRATED.

EXAMPLE:
"I CAN'T HANDLE ANY MORE BAD NEWS TODAY. "

DESCRIPTION:
DEPICTS A FACE WITH LARGE, SHINY EYES, SUGGESTING PLEADING OR BEGGING. IT CONVEYS A SENSE OF VULNERABILITY OR SINCERITY.

EXAMPLE:
"CAN WE PLEASE GET ICE CREAM? "

DESCRIPTION:

DISPLAYS A TEAR ROLLING DOWN FROM ONE EYE, SHOWING SADNESS, DISAPPOINTMENT, OR MILD GRIEF.

EXAMPLE:

"I'M REALLY GOING TO MISS YOU. "

DESCRIPTION:

A MORE INTENSE VERSION OF THE CRYING FACE, THIS EMOJI HAS STREAMS OF TEARS. REPRESENTS STRONG FEELINGS OF SADNESS OR DESPAIR.

EXAMPLE:

"I CAN'T BELIEVE THE SERIES IS OVER! "

DESCRIPTION:

SHOWS A FACE THAT IS PUFFING OUT STEAM FROM ITS NOSTRILS, DEPICTING ANGER OR FRUSTRATION

EXAMPLE:

"WHEN PEOPLE DON'T KEEP THEIR PROMISES... "

DESCRIPTION:
REPRESENTS FEELINGS OF ANGER OR ANNOYANCE.

EXAMPLE:
"I TOLD HIM NOT TO TOUCH MY THINGS! "

DESCRIPTION:
CONVEYS MORE INTENSE ANGER COMPARED TO THE ANGRY FACE EMOJI. IT'S OFTEN ASSOCIATED WITH FRUSTRATION, DISAPPOINTMENT, OR BEING UPSET.

EXAMPLE:
"THIS IS THE LAST STRAW! "

DESCRIPTION:
DEPICTS A FACE WITH SYMBOLS COVERING THE MOUTH, INDICATING STRONG FEELINGS OF ANGER, FRUSTRATION, OR SWEARING.

EXAMPLE:
"WHEN YOU STUB YOUR TOE ON THE CORNER OF THE BED. "

DESCRIPTION:

REPRESENTS FEELINGS OF SHOCK, DISBELIEF, OR BEING OVERWHELMED TO THE POINT WHERE IT FEELS LIKE ONE'S HEAD MIGHT EXPLODE.

EXAMPLE:

"I JUST FOUND OUT I WON THE LOTTERY! "

DESCRIPTION:

SHOWS A FACE TURNING PINK, INDICATING EMBARRASSMENT, SURPRISE, OR MILD SHAME.

EXAMPLE:

"I CAN'T BELIEVE I JUST SAID THAT OUT LOUD. 😳

DESCRIPTION:

REPRESENTS FEELINGS OF BEING OVERHEATED, EITHER DUE TO HIGH TEMPERATURES OR FROM A STRESSFUL OR UNCOMFORTABLE SITUATION.

EXAMPLE:

"THE SUMMER HEAT TODAY IS UNBEARABLE! "

DESCRIPTION:
REPRESENTS FEELING COLD, OFTEN DUE TO CHILLY WEATHER OR A COLD ENVIRONMENT.

EXAMPLE:
"I FORGOT MY JACKET, AND NOW I'M FREEZING! "

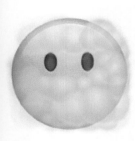

DESCRIPTION:
DEPICTS A FACE SURROUNDED BY CLOUDS, INDICATING FEELINGS OF CONFUSION, DAZE, OR DAYDREAMING.

EXAMPLE:
"I HAVE NO IDEA WHAT'S GOING ON RIGHT NOW. "

DESCRIPTION:
REPRESENTS FEELINGS OF SHOCK, FEAR, OR INTENSE SURPRISE. IT'S LIKE THE VISUAL REPRESENTATION OF THE PHRASE "HOME ALONE FACE."

EXAMPLE:
"THAT JUMP SCARE IN THE MOVIE GOT ME LIKE "

DESCRIPTION:

SHOWS A FACE THAT'S CLEARLY ALARMED OR SCARED, OFTEN USED IN SITUATIONS OF SUDDEN REALIZATION OR GENUINE CONCERN.

EXAMPLE:

"DID I LEAVE THE OVEN ON AT HOME? "

DESCRIPTION:

REPRESENTS NERVOUSNESS OR ANXIETY, OFTEN ABOUT A SPECIFIC EVENT OR SITUATION. THE DROP OF SWEAT EMPHASIZES THE STRESS OR CONCERN.

EXAMPLE:

"WAITING FOR MY EXAM RESULTS LIKE... "

DESCRIPTION:

PORTRAYS MIXED FEELINGS OF RELIEF AND SADNESS. IT CAN ALSO INDICATE SWEATING FROM HEAT OR EXERTION.

EXAMPLE:

"THE STORM IS OVER, BUT THE DAMAGE IS DONE "

DESCRIPTION:
REPRESENTS STRESS, HARD WORK, OR DISCOMFORT, EITHER DUE TO A CHALLENGING SITUATION OR PHYSICAL EXERTION.

EXAMPLE:
"JUST FINISHED A TWO-HOUR WORKOUT. "

DESCRIPTION:
CONVEYS WARMTH AND FRIENDLINESS, AS IF GIVING SOMEONE A HUG. CAN ALSO SHOW EMPATHY OR COMFORT.

EXAMPLE:
"I'M HERE FOR YOU, ALWAYS. "

DESCRIPTION:
INDICATES DEEP THOUGHT OR CONSIDERATION. OFTEN USED WHEN PONDERING A QUESTION OR REFLECTING ON SOMETHING.

EXAMPLE:
"SHOULD I HAVE PIZZA OR PASTA FOR DINNER? "

DESCRIPTION:

EXPRESSES A CHEEKY OR PLAYFUL FORM OF SURPRISE, OFTEN USED WHEN SOMEONE HAS SAID SOMETHING FUNNY, SASSY, OR MILDLY INAPPROPRIATE BUT IN A LIGHT-HEARTED MANNER.

EXAMPLE:

"I PROBABLY SHOULDN'T HAVE SAID THAT, BUT IT WAS TOO FUNNY! 🤭"

DESCRIPTION:

INDICATES A REQUEST FOR SILENCE OR SECRECY. THE FINGER OVER THE LIPS SIGNALS "BE QUIET" OR "KEEP IT A SECRET".

EXAMPLE:

"LET'S KEEP THIS BETWEEN US. 🤫"

DESCRIPTION:

THE PEACH EMOJI DEPICTS A ROUND, FLESHY, ORANGE PEACH. IT IS MAINLY USED TO REPRESENT A BUTT.

EXAMPLE:

"EVERY TIME I SEE YOU WALK AWAY, I JUST MELT. 🍑"

DESCRIPTION:
A FACE WITH A LONG NOSE, REMINISCENT OF PINOCCHIO. IT'S USED TO SUGGEST THAT SOMEONE IS LYING OR BEING UNTRUTHFUL.

EXAMPLE:
"I SWEAR I DIDN'T EAT THE LAST COOKIE. "

DESCRIPTION:
REPRESENTS SILENCE, SPEECHLESSNESS, OR A DESIRE TO REMAIN NEUTRAL AND NOT COMMENT.

EXAMPLE:
"WHEN YOU HAVE NOTHING TO SAY... "

DESCRIPTION:
INDICATES A NEUTRAL SENTIMENT. NEITHER HAPPY NOR SAD, OFTEN USED TO CONVEY INDIFFERENCE OR MILD IRRITATION.

EXAMPLE:
"WELL, THAT HAPPENED. "

DESCRIPTION:

SOMETIMES IT IS USED AS A COMPLIMENT OR A SYNONYM FOR "SEXY", "BEAUTIFUL", AND "HOT"

EXAMPLE:

"YOU LOOK GREAT TODAY! "

DESCRIPTION:

SHOWS A LACK OF EMOTION OR REACTION, OFTEN USED TO CONVEY BOREDOM, FRUSTRATION, OR FEELING UNIMPRESSED.

EXAMPLE:

"ANOTHER FLAT TIRE? GREAT. "

DESCRIPTION:

REPRESENTS A CRINGE OR AWKWARD FEELING. THI EMOJI IS OFTEN USED WHEN SOMEONE IS NERVOUS OR EMBARRASSED.

EXAMPLE:

"ACCIDENTALLY CALLED MY BOSS 'MOM'. "

DESCRIPTION:
EXPRESSES DISBELIEF, ANNOYANCE, OR THE SENTIMENT OF "HERE WE GO AGAIN."

EXAMPLE:
"HE'S LATE FOR THE THIRD TIME THIS WEEK. 🙄"

DESCRIPTION:
INDICATES SURPRISE, SHOCK, OR BEING RENDERED SPEECHLESS.

EXAMPLE:
"I DIDN'T EXPECT THAT PLOT TWIST! "

DESCRIPTION:
REPRESENTS FEELINGS OF SHOCK, DISMAY, OR MILD SADNESS.

EXAMPLE:
"I CAN'T BELIEVE THEY CANCELLED MY FAVORITE SHOW. 🙁"

DESCRIPTION:
REPRESENTS FEELINGS OF PAIN, SHOCK, OR DISMAY
IT'S LIKE A MIX OF SURPRISE AND SADNESS.

EXAMPLE:
"JUST FOUND OUT MY FAVORITE
CAFÉ IS CLOSING DOWN. 😣"

DESCRIPTION:
INDICATES SURPRISE OR ASTONISHMENT. IT CAN
ALSO SHOW THAT SOMEONE IS IMPRESSED.

EXAMPLE:
"THEY'RE GIVING AWAY FREE ICE CREAM? 😮"

DESCRIPTION:
REPRESENTS A STRONGER SENSE OF SHOCK OR
AMAZEMENT THAN THE "FACE WITH OPEN MOUTH."

EXAMPLE:
"DID YOU SEE THAT METEOR JUST NOW? 😲"

DESCRIPTION:
INDICATES FEELING SLEEPY OR BORED. USED WHEN SOMETHING IS TIRING OR UNINTERESTING.

EXAMPLE:
"THIS MEETING IS DRAGGING ON. "

DESCRIPTION:
REPRESENTS DEEP SLEEP. OFTEN USED TO CONVEY THE ACT OF SLEEPING OR THE DESIRE TO GO TO BED.

EXAMPLE:
"GOODNIGHT EVERYONE, I'M OFF TO DREAMLAND. "

DESCRIPTION:
SHOWS A FACE WITH DROOL DRIPPING FROM ONE SIDE OF THE MOUTH. USED TO REPRESENT A DESIRE FOR SOMETHING, TYPICALLY FOOD.

EXAMPLE:
"EVERY TIME I SEE THAT CHOCOLATE CAKE, I'M LIKE... "

DESCRIPTION:
REPRESENTS FEELINGS OF TIREDNESS OR BEING
READY FOR BED, BUT NOT YET SLEEPING. IT ALSO
CAN CONVEY FEELING RELIEVED OR CONTENT.

EXAMPLE:
"LONG DAY AT WORK. READY TO HIT THE SACK.

DESCRIPTION:
REPRESENTS RELIEF OR A SIGH. IT CAN ALSO BE
USED TO INDICATE SOMEONE IS FEELING WORN
OUT.

EXAMPLE:
"FINISHED MY FINAL EXAMS! 😮‍💨"

DESCRIPTION:
REPRESENTS FEELING OUT OF SORTS, DIZZY, OR
DISORIENTED. IT MAY ALSO SIGNIFY BEING AMAZED
TO THE POINT OF SPEECHLESSNESS.

EXAMPLE:
"I SPUN AROUND TOO MANY TIMES AND NOW I'M AL
."

DESCRIPTION:
CONVEYS A SENSE OF BEING STUNNED, DAZED, OR OVERWHELMED. CAN ALSO INDICATE FEELING "OUT OF IT" OR NOT FULLY PRESENT.

EXAMPLE:
"AFTER READING THAT MIND-BENDING BOOK, I FELT ."

DESCRIPTION:
REPRESENTS A SECRET OR SOMETHING THAT SHOULDN'T BE SPOKEN ABOUT. THIS EMOJI MEANS "I WON'T SAY ANYTHING" OR "MY LIPS ARE SEALED."

EXAMPLE:
"I PROMISED NOT TO SPILL THE BEANS. "

DESCRIPTION:
SHOWS A FACE WITH UNEVEN EYES AND A WAVY MOUTH. REPRESENTS FEELINGS OF EXHAUSTION, BEING OVERWHELMED, INTOXICATED, OR SLIGHTLY OUT OF IT.

EXAMPLE:
"TRIED TO STAY UP FOR 48 HOURS STRAIGHT... BAD IDEA. "

DESCRIPTION:
REPRESENTS FEELINGS OF SICKNESS, DISGUST, OR GENERAL AVERSION TO SOMETHING.

EXAMPLE:
"TRIED THAT NEW WEIRD FLAVOR OF ICE CREAM... NEVER AGAIN. 🤢"

DESCRIPTION:
CONVEYS STRONG LEVELS OF DISGUST, EITHER PHYSICAL (LIKE WANTING TO THROW UP) OR METAPHORICAL (LIKE AN AVERSION TO SOMETHING).

EXAMPLE:
"JUST SAW THE MOST DISGUSTING SCENE IN A MOVIE. 🤮"

DESCRIPTION:
REPRESENTS SNEEZING OR BEING SICK. IT CAN ALSO CONVEY THAT SOMEONE IS FEELING UNDER THE WEATHER.

EXAMPLE:
"COLD SEASON HAS ME LIKE... 🤧"

DESCRIPTION:
DEPICTS A FACE WEARING A MEDICAL MASK, USED TO REPRESENT ILLNESS OR TO CONVEY THE MESSAGE OF PROTECTING ONESELF FROM GERMS OR POLLUTION.

EXAMPLE:
"STAYING SAFE DURING FLU SEASON. "

DESCRIPTION:
REPRESENTS BEING ILL OR FEELING UNWELL.

EXAMPLE:
"CAME DOWN WITH A FEVER TODAY. "

DESCRIPTION:
CONVEYS FEELING PHYSICALLY HURT, EITHER DUE TO A MINOR INJURY OR EMOTIONAL PAIN.

EXAMPLE:
"TRIPPED AND TOOK A NASTY FALL. "

DESCRIPTION:
REPRESENTS THE FEELING OF BEING RICH, WINNIN
MONEY, OR HAVING A STRONG DESIRE FOR WEALTH
OFTEN USED WHEN TALKING ABOUT MONEY-MAKIN
OPPORTUNITIES OR THE DESIRE FOR LUXURY.

EXAMPLE:
"JUST GOT MY BONUS! GOING SHOPPING. "

DESCRIPTION:
OFTEN REFERRED TO AS THE "COWBOY EMOJI," IT
CONVEYS FEELINGS OF ADVENTURE, EXCITEMENT
OR BEING IN A FUN, CHEEKY MOOD.

EXAMPLE:
"HEADING TO THE RODEO LIKE... "

DESCRIPTION:
REPRESENTS MISCHIEVOUS OR DEVILISH BEHAVIOR
IT'S OFTEN USED TO CONVEY PLAYFUL MISCHIEF O
CHEEKINESS.

EXAMPLE:
"PLANNING A LITTLE PRANK FOR APRIL FOOLS'
DAY. 😈"

DESCRIPTION:

DEPICTS A DEVILISH CHARACTER BUT IN A MORE UPSET OR FRUSTRATED MANNER. CAN BE USED TO EXPRESS MILD ANGER OR ANNOYANCE.

EXAMPLE:

"WHEN SOMEONE TAKES THE LAST SLICE OF PIZZA WITHOUT ASKING. 😈"

DESCRIPTION:

CAN BE USED LITERALLY TO DESCRIBE A CLOWN OR METAPHORICALLY TO DESCRIBE SOMEONE ACTING FOOLISH OR MAKING JOKES.

EXAMPLE:

"YOU THINK YOU CAN TRICK ME WITH THAT? NICE TRY, CLOWN. 🤡"

DESCRIPTION:

REPRESENTS FECES BUT IS COMMONLY USED IN A PLAYFUL MANNER TO DESCRIBE A "CRAPPY" SITUATION OR TO DENOTE SOMETHING THAT'S SEEN AS SILLY OR UNIMPORTANT.

EXAMPLE:

"MY DAY'S BEEN 💩 HOW ABOUT YOURS?"

DESCRIPTION:
OFTEN USED AROUND HALLOWEEN OR TO DESCRIBE SOMETHING SPOOKY, BUT CAN ALSO BE USED IN A PLAYFUL CONTEXT TO DENOTE "GHOSTING" SOMEONE OR FEELING INVISIBLE.

EXAMPLE:
"GEARING UP FOR A SPOOKY MOVIE NIGHT! 👻"

DESCRIPTION:
REPRESENTS DEATH OR DANGER, BUT IS FREQUENTLY USED IN A HUMOROUS OR EXAGGERATED WAY TO CONVEY "I'M DEAD" AS IN FINDING SOMETHING EXTREMELY FUNNY OR BEING OVERWHELMED.

EXAMPLE:
"THAT JOKE WAS SO FUNNY, I'M 💀."

DESCRIPTION:
REPRESENTS EXTRATERRESTRIAL LIFE. CAN BE USED TO DESCRIBE SOMETHING OUT OF THIS WORLD OR FEELING LIKE AN OUTSIDER.

EXAMPLE:
"THIS NEW GAME IS 👽 LEVEL GOOD."

DESCRIPTION:
REPRESENTS A ROBOT OR SOMETHING MECHANICAL. ALSO USED METAPHORICALLY TO DESCRIBE SOMEONE ACTING WITHOUT EMOTIONS OR BEING "ROBOTIC" IN THEIR ACTIONS.

EXAMPLE:
"RUNNING ON AUTOPILOT TODAY. 🤖"

DESCRIPTION:
REPRESENTS HALLOWEEN AND SPOOKY FESTIVITIES.

EXAMPLE:
"CAN'T WAIT HALLOWEEN 🎃 THIS YEAR!"

DESCRIPTION:
IT'S FREQUENTLY USED AS A DOUBLE ENTENDRE TO REPRESENT MALE GENITALIA DUE TO ITS SHAPE.

EXAMPLE:
"HOW WAS YOUR DATE YESTERDAY? "

Printed in Great Britain
by Amazon

41833256R00025